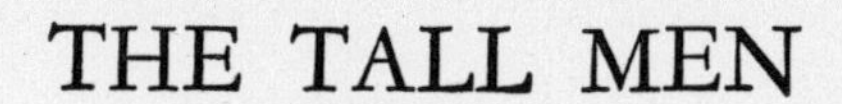

THE TALL MEN

BY

DONALD DAVIDSON

Author of 'An Outland Piper'

BOSTON AND NEW YORK
HOUGHTON MIFFLIN COMPANY
The Riverside Press Cambridge
1927

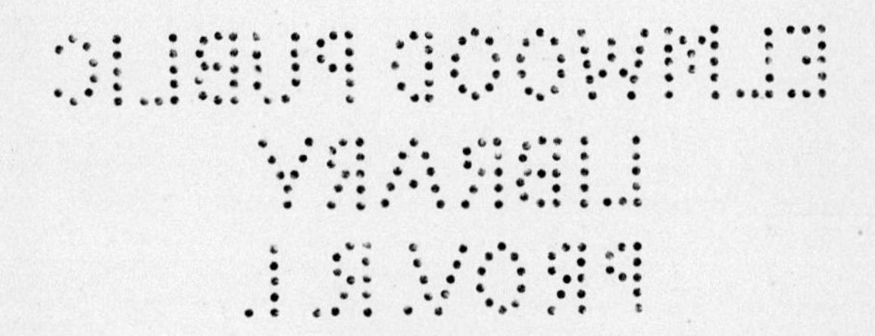

The Riverside Press
CAMBRIDGE · MASSACHUSETTS
PRINTED IN THE U.S.A.

DEDICATED TO
MY FATHER
WILLIAM BLUFORD DAVIDSON
AND TO THE MEMORY OF
MY MOTHER
ELMA WELLS DAVIDSON

'Nay,' sayd the lord Persë,
'I tolde it the beforne,
That I wolde never yeldyde be
to no man of a woman born.'

Acknowledgment is made to the Poetry Society of South Carolina for permission to reprint 'Fire on Belmont Street,' which was chosen as their Southern Prize Poem for 1926.

CONTENTS

PROLOGUE

THE LONG STREET

PACING the long street where is no summer
But only burning summer — looking for spring
That is not, spring that will not be here
But with its blunt remembrancer and friend,
Its blunt friend Death . . . Pacing the long street
That ends with winter that will never be
Winter as men would say it . . . Thinking of autumn
What but a few blown leaves and the biting smoke
That feeds on all of these till autumn is not
Autumn? The seasons, even the seasons wither,
And all is mingled with a chaff of time
Till I must wonder, pacing the long street,
If anything in this vague inconceivable world
Can end, lie still, be set apart, be named.

Yet I would name and set apart from time
One sudden face, built from a clay and spittle

Ancient as time, stubborn as these square cliffs
Of brick and steel that here enclose my steps.

The grass cannot remember; trees cannot
Remember what once was here. But even so,
They too are here no longer. Where is the grass?
Only the blind stone roots of the dull street
And the steel thews of houses flourish here,
And the baked curve of asphalt, smooth, trodden,
Covers dead earth that once was quick with grass.
Snuffling the ground with acrid breath the motors
Fret the long street. Steel answers steel. Dust whirls.
Skulls hurry past with the pale flesh yet clinging
And a little hair. Fevered bones under clean
Linen. Aimless knuckles of bones
Within buttoned gloves waving to eyeless sockets:
"Good day, old friend! Good day, my girl! Good-bye!
So long, old man!"

So long, forever so.
Forever, night after night, to say good-bye
Across the portals of an iron age

And close the ivory gate with hopeless stare
Down the long street and up and down again.
Again, old man? How shall we meet again . . .
To-night, for lights bloom up uncertainly for us,
Or in this dead commingled smoke and dark take leave
Of dead men under a pall, nameless and choked?

THE TALL MEN

It was a hunter's tale that rolled like wind
Across the mountains once, and the tall men came
Whose words were bullets. They, by the Tennessee waters,
Talked with their rifles bluntly and sang to the hills
With a whet of axes. Smoke arose where smoke
Never had been before. The Red Man's lodges
Darkened suddenly with a sound of mourning.
Bison, cropping the blue-grass, raised their heads
To a strange wind that troubled them. The deer
Leaped in the thicket, vainly loathing the death
That stung without arrows. The great bear, hungry for
cattle,
Nudged the rough logs of an unyielding pen
And returned no more, having seen the fangs
Of the snarling dogs and the bright knife of the hunter.
Looks were all westward, I have heard, and feet,
Firm in moccasins after the Indian fashion,
Moved with keen presence like the quiet stir
Of a ravenous spring. The lips of hunters awoke

With rumor of far lands till Carolina
Firesides were restless, till the tall Virginians hated
The easy warmth of houses, the too-many-peopled
World. In twos and threes the tall men
Strode in the valleys. Their palisades were pitched
In the Cumberland hills. They brought their teeming wives
To rock the hickory cradles and to mould
Bullets for words that said: "Give way, Red Man.
You have lived long enough. The seed is sown and covered
Which like the dragon's-teeth in a new soil
Shall sprout full-armed in tall men who fight
With a lazy smile, speaking from long rifles."

Something (call it civilization) crept
Across the mountains once, and left me here
Flung up from sleep against the breakfast table
Like numb and helpless driftwood. Through the trees
Where summer morning grows with a threat of drouth
I look back on the centuries (not quite two),
Rustling the morning paper and watching the clock.
On upper Sixth . . . some negroes . . . yesterday
Dug up old bones . . . and trash . . . while excavating . . .

Fundaments for the latest Towers of Babel!
An Indian grave, the state geologist says,
With beads and bear-tooth necklace and a few
Chipped flints and pots. Another grave?
What's that to me who have my teeth to wash
And a cigarette to light before I catch
A car at eight-fifteen with a paper folded
Neatly in my coat pocket. I must remember
Always to look before crossing. A man was killed
On this historic corner the other day
For failing to look while civilization crept
Upon him with rubber wheels and a stench of gas.
But here no Indians lurk. The motorman
Knows perfectly what I want. The prisoned air,
Steel, and electricity obey his wrist,
And my soft proud body is borne on the smooth
Parallel rails into a city hoarse
With nine o'clock which brings the swivel-chair
And to the hungry brain the pelt of typewriters.

Some sort of a battle, would you call it, where
Words pass for bullets, dabbed in a scribble of ink?

THE TALL MEN

Now here the hero sprawls while a little man
Purrs in a patent tone of voice and a sleek
Copyrighted smile. He has a Northern way
Of clipping his words, and with an inevitable curve
Of an arm in a business suit reveals cigars
In the tribal code. Then we are wreathed in smoke
Like friends. He says: "You are so tall, you men,
You Tennesseans. I've never seen so many
Tall fellows riding in elevators.
What makes you then so tall? Is it the cornbread
And the buttermilk, or is it in the air,
Or is it having to climb so many hills
That makes you stretch your legs?"

Why, since you ask,

Tallness is not in what you eat or drink
But in the seed of man. And I am minded
(Remembering an Indian grave) to speak
As only I can speak of what I am,
What were the loins that begot me, what the breasts
That suckled me in danger, what the blood
Running rebelliously within me still

Of the tall men who walked here when there were
No easy roads for walking or for riding. . . .

The curve of Mill Creek with its throat of moonlight
Dazzled McCrory's eyes and made him dream
Of how a girl's neck looks against the gray
Homespun at candle-lighting time.
Such fleshly thoughts were not his business,
And yet he thought them, gazing below his perch
At the dark logs of the station and the roof
Beneath which Phœbe slept, with her warm neck
Curved on a pillow. Outside it was cold
And tedious bother watching for the Indians
Who had not come and would not come, perhaps.
For it was already past the full of the moon;
The spies had skinned the country — all for nothing,
If he was any judge. It was plumb queer,
The way Buchanan had his dander up
And kept fifteen strong men away from harvest,
Waiting for Creeks and Cherokees to come.
Why couldn't he take the word of Indian fighters
Who'd never yet guessed wrong? McCrory's feet

Ached with the cold. He scuffed them on the bark.
The sentinel in the opposite shadow leaned
Lazily in his tower. The leaves of autumn
Roared and drooped, and the moon was midnight high.

A spatter of hoofbeats in the bottom-grass
Broke upward to the fort. McCrory jerked
Awake like a cat and saw a straggling herd
Of darting cattle, wild and snorting, crash
Through the plum-thickets and blackberry bushes. What
Had startled them? Maybe a prowling bear
Or a nosy wild-cat? Maybe something else,
A nosy Cherokee or Creek? His rifle
Slid on the steady logs. McCrory peered.

And there they were, the painted devils, slinking
Across a patch of sedge. His rifle split
September midnight dead in two. He saw
A feathered topknot sag and crumple. God!
A good shot! Now to get reloaded quickly,
Ram and fire again while in the bare
Closure of palisades the tall forms raced
Madly with rifles tall as a man to station,

Speaking hotly into the moonlight greetings
One-syllabled that were not gentle. Then
The hunters remembered their boasts. And useless they
        thought
Was the life on earth of the Creek and the Cherokee.
Unacata drooped already with neck
Bubbling his blood. And Talotiskee tripped
Like steer beneath the axe when the bullet grunted
Home in his breast. Easy shooting, they said,
Laying a cheek against the stock and slowly
Drawing a bead. They felt the steel grow hot
Against their hard palms, looked and fired and looked
While Sally Buchanan ducked beneath the loopholes,
Bringing them powder and ball and pouring whiskey
Out of a gourd. The bullets ripped and smacked
Around lean heads that had forgot to flinch,
And eyes that spotted flashes in the bush.
But now a torch lunged forward on the arm
Of Kiachatallee. The chief whose life was charmed
Despised the white men's rifles as he ran.
Leaping as a deer leaps, climbing as a squirrel
Climbs, he topped the flat low roof

And poked the flame against the tindery bark
While the lead spattered and the red devils whooped.
The hunters cursed and fretted when their bullets
Fell weak against the Indian medicine.
They could not draw a bead. McCrory said,
By God, I'll get him yet! and climbed his perch
Again, hurling his cap across the logs
And spitting for luck. He laid the barrel steady,
Smoothly gripping the trigger. The Indian jumped
Like a stricken deer. His falling arc of flame
Dashed on the groundward logs. McCrory strained
In an awkward cramp to get a second bead
While the dark form was scuffling desperately
To blow the dying torch. Then suddenly
The hunters knew the dawn and heard a boom
From northward hills where Nashboro was, and said,
It's Robertson with men and guns. But now,
Softly as night, the Red Men all had gone.

I have not seen the legendary tree
Where D. BOON CILLED A BAR and lightly slept
With one eye open, leathery cheek on rifle.

Another tree I know, a veteran
Of storms and traffic on a city street,
Bulging its muscular trunk in the dreary middle
Of glib macadam, sending its roots in the deep
Stones of the world where earth and Tennessee
Are all the same. The tree divides the stream
Of motors roaring homeward on the hill.
Here, from the Natchez trail, the files of hunters
Warily lounged. And here war-parties met,
Pausing to spy the country, hooting like owls
In the forest twilight. Here I pass with looks
Too reminiscent for a clear impression
Of four-room bungalows fronting a concrete path
That radiates heat. And here I am besieged
By ghosts and shadows much too tall to be
The spirits of the little men who died
Respectably last week in a private hospital.
And I must let them speak as they know how . . .

JOHN SEVIER

Xavier my name in the Gascon country till
My great-sires came to England, and were called

Sevier in the rough English speech, but lost
No chivalry of their ancient name. I loved
The praise of men in hunting-shirts who cheered
For Nolichucky Jack at Watauga Old Fields
And followed me through night and the dripping forest
To King's Mountain. We were the backwoods hornets
Crowding the rocky slopes and buzzing death
To that gaudy lion, Ferguson. Elsewhere
It was the same. The sword of the Lord and of Gideon
In my hands smote the Indian villages
To dust and ashes till I lived in peace,
Governing my country, loving my Bonny Kate,
And seeking the praise of men. But where are they?
Where are Shelby and Campbell? Where is Cosby?
Where are the rifles and the lean hunters
Who strode the long trail with me? Have they left
No tall sons to hate what should be hated
And love what should be loved — the praise of men
Speaking with quiet eyes behind long rifles?

ANDREW JACKSON

What makes men live but honor? I have felt
The bullet biting next to my heart and yet
I kept my life for honor's sake and killed
My enemy. And what else was the fire
That fed my sickly body when I shamed
The Tennesseans into victory
At Horseshoe Bend? What was it then but honor
That blazed too hot for British regulars
At New Orleans? Then all the people knew
That I was of their breed and trusted me.
Cowards and lies and little men will pass,
But honor, by the Eternal, will endure.

DAVID CROCKETT

The corn-shuckings and square dances, the fiddles,
The barrels of gin and whiskey, the jerked venison,
Juicy bear meat, hot corn pone, molasses,
And the girls giggling in corners — those are the
things
That make life merry. But there came a time
When I neglected them all, and we made merry

(My Betsey and I) at a different kind of party,
Playing with powder and ball at the Alamo.
I regret nothing, not even the lies and jokes
I told in Congress. But what is this I hear?
Tennesseans, have you forgotten the songs
Of Old Zip Coon and Turkey in the Straw?

These are the words of ghosts. I was not there,
At Talledega, Horseshoe Bend, King's Mountain,
Not at Suwannee, Mobile, or Pensacola
In days when men were tall. I have not eaten
Acorns to still my hunger or followed the war-path
After a fiery leader tough as the hickory.
I have not heard the cry of the owl at night
With dreadful understanding. I have not seen
A friend plunge, furred with arrows, across his plough
Or heard the scream of a woman snatched from the hearth
By painted warriors. And when it was misty dawn
I was not by the ragged breastworks, priming my rifle,
Hearing the British drums beat. I have not sung
Old songs or danced old tunes. I have read a book.

I have loitered by graves. I have trod old floors,
Tiptoed through musty rooms and glanced at letters
Spread under glass and signed *Yr Obt Servant*,
And wistfully conned old platitudes in stone.
But shall I say the praise of men, bright honor,
The songs of my own race and the ways of fighters
Are something read in a book only, or graven
Only in stone and not in the hearts of men?

Speaking with words for bullets politely now
I move on rubber heels dividing parallel grooves
On the swept sidewalk. I with an evening paper
Folded neatly in my coat pocket salute the tree
And walk, a veteran of storms and traffic, home,
Where windows bloom with mellow lights against
A square slab of buildings. This is dusk
Where tall men humped on cushioned seats glide home
Impatiently. Feet in immaculate leather,
Silken-cased, urge down the throttle gently,
Speeding with effort only of ankle and wrist.
Seven o'clock in the twentieth century is
The hour of supper, not the hour of prayer,

And something (call it civilization) turns
A switch; a fan hums pianissimo,
Blowing old ghosts to outer darkness where
The bones of tall men lie in the Tennessee earth.

THE SOD OF BATTLE-FIELDS

"By the Battery Road," he said, and veered the wheel
With casual wrist among the westward hills
Where all the neglected ghosts launch up in vain
Pleadings unrecognized. Here once of old
The westering sun called blood upon the hills
While men in gray reeled backward from the charge,
And saw the stubborn cannoneers, the dogged
Mouths of the guns through settling smoke, and dropped
To breathe in scattered ranks until despair
Herded them on like the ragged drift of autumn
Tossed by a northern wind. The Battery Road?
Now but a glimpse of naked trees and a sere
Whirl of meadows, flashed on the speeding eyes,
Not yet opaque while phantoms trouble them,
Or fetches rouse the slumbering brain, until
The pageant of old wounds and gallantries
Beats for remembrance, quick in the startled mind.

Old men remember this who creep to the sun
In the winter of a time that heeds them not.

They are the proof of ancient differences
Not yet committed to the grave. They warm
Their bones with names that are not names to them
But panoplied moments, exultations made
Visible in the flesh that woke their banners.
This one has followed Lee. He has clutched the mane
Of the gray charger and wept farewell. He knows
Lee was the grandest face that ever looked
Victory to the conquered. This one has cheered
For Stonewall Jackson, riding the long gray lines
At Fredericksburg where ranks were steel. Then came
The lunge through Wilderness woods, the fatal moon
Of Chancellorsville, the waving plume of Stuart.
Another dropped at Chickamauga, felled
By the Bloody Pond. Another was taken at Vicks-
burg.
Another galloped from Donelson with Forrest
And never was taken. Another remembers groups
Of skirmishers that light as hounds advanced
On Little Round Top. This one has seen the dead
Peaceful as sleep on Shiloh field by the river . . .
Laughter of a girl, uplifting at a gate

A face of love in sixty-three . . . the dust
Of cavalry gone from a Tennessee road forever.

These remember, and some forget. But here
Was the place of battle. You who have never known
The scour and pierce of battle may only remember
Moments by names, places by monuments,
But I who was born by the battle-fields cannot
Escape a sorrow that dwells, a valor that lingers,
A hope that spoke on lips now still. It is
A fey place, haunted and old with tales
That I have heard and will not soon forget.

The Yankees came at night, my grandmother said,
Plundering the stables, leading the horses out.
They said, *Why, you won't need* your *old barn now,*
And so we'll burn it.
Chickens stirred in the cedars,
Stretching their necks at this unusual glare.

She put her nose against the kitchen window
With the other little girls in flannel nightgowns,

Hearing the horses stamp and whinny, hearing
Her mother sob, hearing the rocking-chair creak
Back and forth like a dull patient dream.

"Mother, if I was a man and had a gun . . .
Mother, if Jim Ezell was here he wouldn't let
The Yankees burn our barn, would he, Mother?"

Then out of the back yard hedge a sudden row
Of eight men in blue with Yankee feet
Violating the porch. Eight men with whiskey-breaths
Bashed into the silence across the carpets, poking
Their long bayonets under the beds and the sofa.
One with a stubby beard and woolly eyebrows
Above a fat chin stuck his Yankee bayonet
Right at a little girl in a flannel nightgown,
Laughing in a whiskey guttural.

"Shucks, I'm not afraid
Of you . . . You're nothing but a damn Yankee!"

Then, many days after, the throb of guns
Repeating their murmur dully from Murfreesboro,

Until dusk without news. Another dawn,
Another day of faint long pounding.
"Mother,
Is it a battle? Mother, is Uncle Paul
Shooting the Yankees? Mother, do you reckon
The Yankees will kill Uncle Paul?"

And there was a tale of Jim Ezell and the Yankees,
How he licked ten of them — fifty, maybe —
All by himself. Oh, he was a Forrest scout
And a Chapel Hill boy, you know. The Yankees
Heard he was lying wounded and in bed
At old Dad Smiley's farm up by the creek.
So they sneaked up, all ten of them (maybe fifty),
And the first thing he knew he was surrounded.
Then Jim rared out of bed like a young colt,
Kicked up his heels, spit bullets in their faces,
That-a-way, this-a-way, lit in his saddle fighting,
Bang through the fence and splash in the creek,
And up the dirt road with his shirt-tail flapping.
The Yankees yelled and shot their guns. No use!
None of your butter-fingered Yankee cavalry

Ever could touch Jim Ezell. It took
Ten Yankees anyhow to lick a Southerner,
Even to make him run.

Another day
(After Chickamauga and the fall
Of Vicksburg, it must have been), my grandmother said,
She was alone in the yard one August evening
Just at twilight, swinging on the gate, maybe.
The noise of horses, pulled to a walk, and metal
Faintly clinking came from up the street
Where voices growled and argued. Then right past her
A troop of Yankee cavalry, some dismounted,
Dragged three men, three boys in country jeans.
One was Len Smiley, grandmother said, the others
She didn't remember. The boys were arguing
Plaintively with the Yankee captain, swearing:
"Why, Captain, we're no spies. You can't mean
You're going to shoot us. We're Confederate soldiers,
Slipped in home for a snack and a change of clothes."
And as they passed the gate Len Smiley said:
"Look here, Captain. I'm no spy. Why there's

Becky Patton. She knows me. She'll tell you
I'm no spy, nor no bushwhacker either."
Roughly the guard, with carbines, dragged them on,
While the captain in Federal blue lounged on his horse
And sucked his moustaches. They took the three young
men,
Lined them up in the middle of the town and shot
them,
Shot them dead right there, those three young fellows,
Just boys, you know, all Chapel Hill boys.
One tried to run. He got across a garden
And over a paling-fence before they stopped him . . .
Full of bullet-holes . . . riddled . . . . The bodies
Lay in three pools of blood until the women
And old men carried them in by candle-light . . .
Dressed them decent . . . buried them.
Riddled . . . the blood lay in pools.

The sod of old battle-fields is washed
Clean of blood. The wind and the rain have worn
Smooth rondures where the jagged breastworks were.
The matted roots of blue-grass hold the earth

Where the young men fell, where the gallant old men
rested
Their tired bones. Some lie under the grass,
Which is victorious here. And little boys
Wrangle on Sundays over the minie-balls,
Much fewer now and hard to find in the grass.
The historic farmhouse where five generals lay
In bloody dignity is pointed out
To strangers. Hood is a one-legged fable
Argued in dusty volumes; Forrest, a name
Remembered by a few old men in gray
Stumbling in the hot sun while the hired band plays
Dixie, and sponsors simper. Heavily the old men
Shoulder their ancient rifles. Ranks are straggling.
Lee is a face, a granite face on a mountain.
And the grandsons of Confederate soldiers learn
About Abe Lincoln, the sad-eyed rail-splitter.
Banks close on his birthday. A few old negroes
Still tip their hats when they meet a white man,
And the years creep slowly by, Lorena.
Flags, bullet-torn, moulder in glass cases
While pneumonia, enemy of old men in gray,

Ravages freely. The U.D.C.'s still meet
Indomitably, despairing of their granddaughters.
The Union is saved. Lee has surrendered forever.
To-day, Lorena, it is forbidden to be
A Southerner. One is American now;
Propounds the pig's conception of the state –
The constitution of, by, for the pig —
Meanwhile pushing his trotters well in the trough.
One goes to the movies, motors on Sunday swiftly
On the baked asphalt:

Yes, this is the Battery Road.
So they say. The battle of Nashville was fought
Somewhere around here. I suppose there's a tablet.
We won't go back to look. The Soldiers' Home? . . .
Off yonder through the trees . . . the new paint factory . . .
A little further on . . . We'll soon be home.

The years creep slowly by, Lorena, till
The sod of the old battle-fields is washed
Clean of all blood. But have I forgotten these
Cool scouts, hidden in a wild-plum thicket,
Once in an autumn dusk near Ewell's Farm,

Perilously quiet, watching the hurried lines
Of Federal blue along the Franklin pike
That crept away while Forrest stamped and fretted?
Have I forgotten powder-blackened mouths
Meeting the ragged flame of enemy rifles
On the Franklin breastworks? Have I forgotten these
Tired eyes of Confederate soldiers lighting
With bitter courage momently at Nashville,
The withered army, the slow retreat, the rain
Falling on huddled shoulders? Have I forgotten
The dead young men whose flesh will not reflower
But in this single bloom which now I pluck,
Weaving it into my spirit as victors weave
A chaplet, gathered from mould, for honor's sake?
This is my body, woven from dead and living,
Given over again to the quick lustration
Of a new moment. This is my body and spirit,
Broken but never tamed, risen from the bloody sod,
Walking suddenly alive in a new morning.

GEOGRAPHY OF THE BRAIN

I

THE modern brain, guarded not only by bone,
Afferent nerves, withering hair, and skin,
Requires the aid of a mystical apparatus
(Weights, levers, motor, steel rods, black boy)
And pyramiding dollars nicely invested
To float in boredom up to the cool fifth floor
And a tiled room. "Forward," says King Brain,
And atrophied muscles push two legs along
The usual carpet. Eleven strides, no more,
For unimportant legs while more important
Hands convey a brief-case or fumble keys,
Or click the light for impatient eyes. The brain
Enters in state its private cave at evening,
Attended by groan of trucks and probable distant
Whirl of chartered dynamos and swish
Of prisoned waters pumped in tubes of lead;
Attended, too, by aluminium, potash,
Dreams of Henry Ford, alembics of Pasteur,
The ingenious soul of Edison, the thousand

Backs and hands of brown and yellow men
In Singapore or Ceylon; attended by
Elaborate giants broidered with ticker-tape
Involved above the smoke at Birmingham
Or perhaps Pittsburgh; attended by bellowing
Of Kansas steers (they go in, animals;
They come out, packages); attended by
The harried eyes of men on subway trains
And pale children staring from tenement windows.
Assisted to a chair (Grand Rapids) by
Two slippers (from St. Louis) bites cigar
(Perhaps Havana) strikes a match (Bellefonte)
Unwrinkles trousers (Massachusetts) leafs
The New York Times (by U.S. Postal service).

And now, dismissing all its ministers
Abruptly as a king should, grows aghast
To hunch in tailored robes of state alone
Upon the apex of a pyramid
Till for rich garniture it summons up
The map of all its native circumstance,
And suddenly it is attended, it is alive.

II

I tell you, I have come a long way, I have come
Down a long street where looking backward is
A chanted roll-call answered in many places
By voices out of the blood. A child keeps asking,
Where was I before I was born? And shall I say,
O questioning son of man, *I do not know*
Where you are now after you are born?
Not yet, for now I speak a different language. Here
In the complex fiber of brain are woven scenes
Meshed thick and deep as hidden roots of grass,
Composing like the grass the sod you are.

III

Over the Southern fields green corn is waving,
Husky and broad of blade. The ranks of corn
Push from the stable earth. The pollen falls,
A yellow life from shaken tassels, piercing
The seed below. Pollen falls in my heart,
A dust of song that sprinkles fruitfulness,
Mellowing like the corn in Southern fields.

For now in the summer dawn there's bottom-land
Where clover must be cut. A boy's hands thrust
Insistent swords of corn-leaves from his face.
Dew falls, a tiny rain. His heavy eyes
Dimly waken above pale morning-glories
Lushly abloom in the dewy shadow of corn.
He pulls a delicate trumpet, hovers to mark
The ornate disk of a passion-flower. The corn
Plucks at his ragged hat. Among jimson-weeds
And straggling blackberry vines he climbs the fence
Along whose crumbling rails neat lizards run
When sun is warm. But now the sun just tips
The ploughed head of Hunter's Knob. Now guineas
Spatter their metal wheels of sound. The creek,
Unheard among deep willow-sprouts and roots
Of silvery sycamore, runs quietly. The field
Waits where the mower already clicks its teeth
And partridges scud whistling. Here are the teams.
Wagons rattle and halt. The haft of a pitchfork
Presses hickory into a youngish palm.
And corn and clover wave over Southern fields,
As in the brain of man where life is stirring.

Have you worked with your hands? Have you tossed the
pungent clover
High with sun-cured stalks into bottomless wagons?
Have you watched the motionless sun? Have you walked
and sweated
Shoulder to shoulder with black men and with white
Among long windrows! Pile the warm hay. Heap
The fat clover high. It is harvest time.
Take this reaping into your body. Take
The numerous life of earth into your brain
With harvest chant while bodies sway and bend —

I'm glad to see . . . the sinkin' sun . . . go down.
Oh, Lawdy!
(Heave yo' pitchfork, heave it, heave that
hay!)
I'll see my gal when Saturday night come aroun'.
Oh, Lawdy, Lawd!
(Don' white-eye, little boy!
Theh's monkeys in this hay. Theh's monkey
sittin'
On yo' shoulder, white boy. Don' let him git
you.)

I'm glad to see . . .
the sinkin' . . .
sun . . .
go down!

IV

I know how twilights come on little towns
When trace-chains jingle homeward. Twilight filters
Cleanly the dross of yellow clapboard houses.
Wooden gates click shut. Between rows of boxwood,
Aromatic for wistful souls, the feet
May drag on moss-grown steps. And loaded trains
Hoot with a long groan on upward grades.
And men sit after supper on the porch
Among the moonflowers. Little boys on the floor
Swing bare feet in the shadows, and distant hills
Rear tree-shapes cut and gnarled against the sky
In fantasies of giants and Indian warriors.

Father, tell us a story. Tell us about
Old times when you were a boy . . .
Oh, yes,

When I was a boy the winters all were snowy,
And it was very cold for little boys
Driving the mule teams into the highest hills
Where the big woods were. There all day we worked
And sawed and split till hands were chapped and sore.
We piled the cordwood high on wagons. Ha!
I tell you we had fires those days. We had
Poplar and hickory logs in the great fireplace. We had
Hoe-cake baked in the ashes and brown new sorghum.
And at Flat Creek in the old home we had
Parties sometimes. Your grandfather was the greatest
Hand for parties. Ha, the songs he could sing,
The tales he could tell, the jokes he could crack!
And I remember the house at corn-shucking time,
With neighbors crowding the doors, and candles lit
On mantels and tables; the turkey, the cake,
The golden pies in the kitchen, the cider barrel;
The fiddles knocking out Old Dan Tucker; the gangs
Of shuffling negroes back of the house, the barn
With mountains of corn piled ready. Two sides
Hollered and whooped as they raced, a-shucking the corn.
I remember. Ha, I have seen it. And I remember

Your great-grandfather, the finest gentleman
That ever lived. Oh, he was finicky
And neat with beard and white moustache
Precisely trimmed. Slender fingers in gloves,
Always in gloves. Feet small, in polished boots.
His thoroughbred horses. He was a thoroughbred
And kept slaves. But that is all gone now,
On account of the War, and I had rather tell you
About Julius Cæsar or Captain John Smith or read
Out of Plutarch's Lives. Or sing you the good old songs
My father used to sing of Barbara Allan,
Old Rosin-My-Beau, or maybe a funny one
Like Frog Went A-Courtin'. Oh, yes, I remember
The Ku Klux riders all in white parading
Around the square at Pulaski, and one who drank
Three buckets of water, saying to frightened negroes,
That's the first drink I've had since the battle of Shiloh.

There's a play on the hill to-night,
A play on the hill to-night
There's a play on the hill to-night.
Don't let the Yankees know it.

The Rebels are my delight,
The Rebels are my delight,
The Rebels are my delight,
Don't let the Yankees know it.

V

The plump black woman wipes the sheeny plates
Deftly, and pads on muted bare black feet
To and fro. Odors of smoke-cured bacon,
Stored onion and strings of peppers float
Under the dingy rafters. The lamp is dim.
It flares, blackening swiftly the glass
Chimney. A sudden breeze bangs doors
And fearful dark is shut without. She hangs
The dishpan on a nail with a mournful clatter,
Saying —

"Hear dat, chile? Hear dat dishpan say
Lawdy, ain't no mo'? Now Mammy's tiahd.
Go 'long chillun. Leave old Mammy rest."

But Aunt Zif, it isn't bedtime yet.
Tell us about the railroad man . . .

"Well, den.

Dere was a woman oncet. She married a man
What wu'ked in de section-gang. She fried his bacon,
Baked his hoe-cake, put it all in his bucket
Ev'y mo'nin' for his snack. One mo'nin'
Dey had words, dem two. He smacked her jaw,
An' she let him go hongry. She said, I ain't
Goneter cook for you. I'll see you dead fust.
At night he ain't come home. Dey said he was gone . . .

Gone, Aunt Zif?

"Gone, honey. You knows what I mean —
Runned over by de train or fell offen de trustle.
An' she cried and cried and nearly cried her eyes out
Twel she 'cided to go to de conjure-man. He said,
You said you'd see him dead fust? Well, den,
You'll hatter see him dead. An' she come home
An' seen de moon thoo de bresh, an' heered a screech-owl
Hollering over by the graveyard. She tuck a bowl
Of mush and milk, she did, an' she sot it down
Right in de co'ner behime de door jist about
Dis time o' night. An' den she sot by de fire
An' holler out real sof' —

Oh, who will come
An' git dis mush an' milk?
An' den she heered
Sumpin' holler, way-off-like, behime
De railroad track and say —
An' I will!
An' so she holler ag'in —
Oh, who will come
An' git dis mush an' milk?
AN' I WILL!
Sumpin' say, a little closeter, behime
De gyarden fence, an' den she say ag'in,
Right sof' an' low —
Oh, who will come
An' git dis mush an' milk?
An' sumpin' say
Right out on de porch out loud:
AN' I WILL!
Who'll come an' git dis mush an' milk? AN' I . . .
Creepin' . . .
Closeter . . .
WHOOO! . . . ."

Oh, mammy, you scared me.
You made me jump. Do the dead come back? Do ha'nts
Live in the graveyard? How can the dead people hear?
"*Dove came down by the foot of my bed,*
The foot of my bed, the foot of my bed.
Dove came down by the foot of my bed,
And he carried the news that I was dead.

"*I'm going away one day before long,*
One day before long, one day before long,
I'm going away one day before long,
And I won't be back till the judgment day."

VI

Black man, when you and I were young together,
We knew each other's hearts. Though I am no longer
A child, and you perhaps unfortunately
Are no longer a child, we still understand
Better maybe than others. There is a wall
Between us, anciently erected. Once
It might have been crossed, men say. But now I cannot
Forget that I was master, and you can hardly

Forget that you were slave. We did not build
The ancient wall, but there it painfully is.
Let us not bruise our foreheads on the wall.

VII

Over the Southern fields a moon of ghosts
Enchants me with old tremulous histories
Of slender hands, proud, smiling lips, and halls
Peopled with fragile beauty. Rich is the land,
Rich and impregnable as this magnolia-bloom
Buried among dark lacquered leaves. Breathe not
Into the golden heart, so deep, of this lush flower
Lest it blacken. Take now only its perfume
Drifting so invisibly, seized for a moment
Only, magic only of moonlight lost
And unassailable love that perished here —
Where moonlight builds tall pillars of a house
Lording a shadowy park. Enter the door
So evidently failing. Here is the stair
Where Lady Miranda walked with futile lips
Gallantly firm. And Captain Prosper here
Was laid in agony by this tall window,

Bleeding from wounds at hands of Caliban,
Mournful as Arthur on the black-draped barge,
And said: *I go, but not to Avalon*
Or any cloud-capped promontory hid
Beyond the eyes of men. The battle's end
Is now my fortune, but this change of state
Confounds me not. A duller magic rules
Until the blood shall speak again.

Here are
In a glass case, pistols that killed a man
For honor's sake. Here music was, and here
Am I beside a failing mansion, looking
For a face I hardly know and thinking I see
The ghosts of gentlemen who died for honor.

VIII

I have come a long way, I tell you. I am attended
(The brain is attended here) by motley splendors:
Dust of battles, creak of wagons, vows
Rotting like antique lace; the smiles of women
Broken like glass; the tales of old men blown
From rheumy beards on the vague wind; silk gowns

Crumbling in attics; ruffled shirts on bones
Of gentlemen in forgotten graves; rifles,
Hunting-shirts, Bibles, looms, and desperate
Flags uncrowned. But is this then to be
Dreadfully attended or have bad dreams? I am
Wherever I go in silent pomp attended
By rivers where I dwelt in good times gone,
The bending Tennessee, the Cumberland
Between high wooded banks, the Father of Waters
Receiving all the westward streams. I go
With speech of the hills, an ancient tongue, on lips
That know no other language. I have taken
Trees for comrades. I acknowledge the oak,
The gray-barked beech, the dark cedar as friends,
But, firmer than all, tough-fibered hickory.
Stranger, smite my breast and feel the hard
Defiance of hickory. Know my attendants, know
My tough friends met by many a traveled road
Whose careless olden songs were chanted in fields
Among long cotton-rows or in the sun
Of corn-thick bottom-land or the grassy sides
Of shelving pastures. Know my haughty attendants,

Proud men quick with a rope or a gun, and quick
With a warm smile. They stay where they are put,
Steady within the modern brain which draws
Attendants grim or beautiful together,
Asking of motley splendor out of the past
A stubborn unity of courage, only
A wall against confusions of this night.

THE FARING

I

FACES gather and merge and build a face
Born as mine from an ancient clay and spittle.
Now changing like a cloud with fire at heart
It is melted, steeled and riven, glamoured with thunder,
Dusted with dust of foreign roads, rained on
By foreign skies, whipped by the shriek of bullets,
Pressed by the stir of marching men to a cast
Less youthful, momently more dark.
Not now the rumored faces of a past
Far distant urge me into being. These
Are faces out of a past that still is present,
Though crusted with time, for still in the twenty-fourth
year
Of manhood I go to war. Still I remember
Faces of men that passed into mine, and scenes
Most terrible or dear, lighted with strange
Glares of old battle-fields and rigid twilights
Watched into darkness on the scarred French hills.

Black letters daubed across a noisy page
Spelled war to men who shook their heads and knew
Only the far-off din of a muffled dream.
But the noise of war came softly on my ears
At first, with a paper crinkling, saying, *Go.*
Accepted. May the twelfth. Report for duty.
Importantly the young man lounged by an open door,
Somewhat abashed before a girl, and said,
With awkward pride, "Well, I've enlisted. Here's
My notice." So until dark they walked
On the Tennessee roads, not saying much.
They stumbled in their speech and already learned
The way of a soldier's love. Parting is first,
Then hope of return, and then perhaps return.

Good-byes there were when good-bye must be stolen
From summoning voices. Later, parting in crowds
With quick touch only of hands, smiles watched
across
A sleet-blown platform. Whispers against the dawn
And keen imperative bugles. Good-bye from trains
Where khaki blurred the windows. One last parting,
Mute, by the topless walls of a giant city

Where parting came forever to many a one,
And feet went down to ships with no returning.

II

In the ship's belly the tall men huddled with guns
And packs tossed on the narrow bunks. Buttoning
blouses,
Setting caps askew smartly, they crowded the rail
On the strange decks wondering. They saw the immense
Vertical lift of the piled buildings sway and whirl as the
ship
Wheeled in the harbor, nosed and let loose by tugs,
Saw the wisps of white on packed ferry-boats and
people
Looking with farewell motions. They saw the sun
Dropping behind New York. They heard the whistles
Roar for the outward bound, for the tanned young faces
(Few over thirty years) looking good-bye
On the camps and the flags. Good-bye, wooded New
World shores,
Houses of their own country. Spume of the green Atlantic
Rushed from the furrowing prow set eastward at last.

Over the Viking road came the Viking blood
Eastward for battle, borne in the Angles' ship,
They who were Angles. They who were Vikings came
Back to the Norman shores, with the Norman sinew
Strong for the oldtime faring, with Norman brow
And the Norman name, fused, molten, changed.
Saxon and Norman came to the elder land,
Jesting in casual tongue, having heard of deeds
Bruited somewhere in France or in Flanders fields.

Liverpool saw a new tide on the Mersey water.
Rumpled khaki poured from the belly of ships,
And the tall men strode in even columns, sluiced
Through the dingy streets where children ran and pointed—

"Why, what's that on your sleeve?"
"A wildcat, sonny,
To scratch the Germans' eyes out."
(A wildcat snarling,
Emblem of western mountains where tall men strode
Once with long rifles. The Decherd rifles are clipped
To a neater weapon. The faces are unchanged.)

The towers of Oxford saw the strangers pass
Lightly on clicking trains. Beyond Senlac
They sped, and only the blood remembered
The narrowing circle of shields, the crunch of axes,
The bitter hail of arrows. By old Southampton,
The port of kings, they camped, having lost or forgotten
A printed letter from GEORGE, R.I., beginning,
"Soldiers of the United States." They crossed
The Channel water indifferently one night,
Snoring in tousled groups. They stamped their feet
On the docks of Havre, and, cursing the dust of camps,
Prepared for inspection on a Norman hill
While a British Major languished. Midnight
Acquainted them with pinching trains on laughable
Small wheels that ticked interminably till dawn,
And they looked out on narrow checkered fields
And poplars feathered against the sky. They chaffed
The sergeant, saying mournfully, "Sergeant!
What is the French for red wine, Sergeant?
What's the word for belly-ache? What's
The English for mademoiselle? What's Arkansas
For big drunk fool? Oh, Sergeant, Sergeant,

Will we have to police this train before we land
Wherever we are going?"

Now they are going
Somewhere in France on roads where Roman eagles
Slanted to meet the Nervii or where
Napoleon, flushed with greetings, galloped from Elba
A hundred years before. The husky guns
Rumbled at twilight from the Western Front.
The slow column poured like moving bronze.
And something (call it civilization) struck
In the latest battle of nations, somewhere in France.

III

Go, stranger, and to Lacadæmon tell
That here, obeying their behest. . . .

We saw
What only those may know who saw at dawn
Beyond Verdun, the tangled flats of Woëvre
Torn with multiple steely beat and the mutter
Of unseen guns tucked in the lonely vast;
Or those who dwelt among the dead on hills
Nameless and lost in Argonne Wood, or crossed

The bridges numerous with blood and lay
Breathless among the shells, but prone and crouching,
Urged the five slim cartridges down with one
Quick press of a thumb, then jammed the hot bolt home;
Let those who know Buzancy, Mont Faucon,
Fossoy, and Grand Pré, Fresnes, and Belleau Wood
Tell how patrols swish by with feet that suck
In the jealous mud of a trench, then clink the wire
And fade unchallenged where the low fog coils;
Or how the candle drips upon the map
As soldiers bunch grim heads and say: *There, there,*
There to-morrow we go. The time is come.
In the cold dugout's silence, the buckling of steel.

Go, stranger, tell, but you can never tell
What you have never known. Simonides
Has told you nothing. This is a fabulous battle
Vast and remote as gulfs beyond Orion,
And alien to your will . . . though you have dreamed
Beside your fire a night in nineteen-eighteen,
Letting staccato headlines droop across your lap
Toward slippered feet. The fire was warm. You dozed.

Then from your nodding sprang awake to hear
The shout of nations in the chimney-blast,
Hollow and wild, from mists beyond the sea,
And saw, before your eyelids blinked awake,
Uprising from the velvet of your dark,
An unknown image, poised and armed for war,
Bold, smeared with earth, the ruddy child of earth,
A soldier of the infantry, who smiled
Behind his tilted rifle, then moved on
Against the wind that smote him with its steel.
Confess the phantasy was true, and still
You have not seen, you will not know or see,
You cannot touch the image that is gone,
And yet there was an image once that lived.

The squadrons of the sky were winging home
Above the shrapnel cloud-puffs, and the guns,
Rousing their throats in Les Éparges, hurled east
Projectile screams that rode the air like howls
Of banshee dreams and struck like demon fists.
But that was overhead. Beneath was cold
And quiet business where McCrory led

The long-shanked riflemen to post, while dusk
Came down upon their crooked ell of trench
Till night prevailed upon them breathing there.
Then each of fifteen men laid out his gear
Ready to hand, the clips of five, the iron
Bulbs of grenades, the rockets, flares and all
The clean smooth cylinders of war. And then
Each man composed his limbs against the frost,
Settled his gun, thumbed back the gliding lock
From safe to ready, for their custom was,
Marching or standing, always to be ready.
They had no mind to sleep.

But in his niche
High up against the parapet, a shelf
Spaded from rock and earth by hands now gone
To some French field, McCrory stood and gazed
Where gazing was, it seemed, so little use
That man as well might sleep. The night was thick
And noiseless in his front, and now the moon
Was past its full and late and weak in rising.
Yet orders still were orders. He must strain
His ear for sounds that death knows how to make,

Immensely trivial where No Man's Land
Poured all its filtered wreck of bush and stone
Into a darkling bowl whose far rim touched
The close pacific stars. Two nights had come
And gone with warning of some enemy raid
Unlaunched as yet from those gray lines where lurked
The stern and quiet foe. To-night the third
Warning pestered the trench, but all was calm.
The phosphorous minutes moved with ticking strides
Upon McCrory's wrist. His feet were cold.
He scuffed them on the frozen shelf and heard
The sentinel in the opposite traverse move
Too restlessly, and cursed him for his noise,
Moving in absent thoughts beyond the sea,
Half-wakefully, remembering how a girl's
Deep eyes commanded his in a land far-off
(And dim as Argos to the Achæan men
Before the hill of Troy, for they had left
Maiden and wife beyond the wine-dark sea).

So huddled in the frost, the riflemen
Endured the pinching hours till from Noire Haie

Five quick convulsive strokes leaped up with roar
Of steel; a long crescendo scream hurled down
Upon the steady trench. They felt the guns'
Hot lips speak toward them, winced for the crash,
and knew
The merging drumbeat of the deft barrage.
Down, down, you men, McCrory yelled, and saw
The dugout's black mouth gulp the bending backs
Till he alone was left. He pressed his side
And head against firm earth that dribbled crumbs of dirt,
Felt at his breast a chain's cool links and drew
The whistle out and ready, pulled the hammer
Back on the wide-mouthed pistol, sent three lights
Bursting to heaven — one green, one red, one green—
And heard the answering batteries multiply
The rage of steel around his deafened head
Which still remembered *Orders! Orders! Orders!*
Wait and pick the moment! Wait and Wait!
Through all eternities of death and flame
While singing fragments whined and plumped their hail.
But now a lull. The great guns lengthened range.
McCrory topped the parapet and peered

While flares made blinding day along the front,
And there they were, the gray-green men, a line
Of forward wrenching shapes, careering, hurling
Lightnings and death about his head. His war-song
Leaped from the whistle, single-clear and shrill
Above the popping night, while in the trench
The tall men rushed to post with guns that spoke
Greetings one-syllabled that were not gentle.
They were not minded to let the strangers live,
For now they remembered the creeping nights, the rain,
The empty vigils and the comrades dead.
Good shooting, said the long-shanked riflemen
Laying the stock against a cheek and coolly
Drawing a bead while hell blazed white around.
They saw the helmets bob and topple, saw
The clenched forms stride and fall, they saw the wire
Sown with clutter of death, they looked and fired
And looked while mad McCrory cried, *By God,*
We'll get them yet, and called for bandoliers
While rushes dwindled.

Now the moon was up,
A sultry peak of light within a ring

Of ominous fog. McCrory stared at the red
Numbness that was his arm, and heard the click
Of bolts along the trench. Then softly as night
The foe had left the field, but many lay
Still where the rifles locked them into slumber.
So many a night there was no mind for sleep,
And many a wish for dawn, till one dawn came
More keen than all. A whisper from the rear
Rolled up a word of fire and filled the night
With pushing steady faces that streamed up
Against the dawn, against the loathly fog,
Against the stranger's bullets where the call
Was *Forward! Forward!* whither captains of men,
Archers and knights of Crécy or the arm
Of a man in a coonskin cap waved back the dark.

I tell you, I have come a long way, I have come
From a world that was into a world that is,
Bringing the strongest part of all I was
Into the moment when all strong things fade
Into a fog of questions. Ask the fog
For comfort? Ask for death! Ask fire to give

Water for parching tongues! Ask rock to feed
The child who sucks a sterile breast! Ask dust
To kiss the desert back to living green!
But once I heard of Marathon, where men
Clutched in the tense of battle, saw great shoulders
Parting the mass, and heard the club of Theseus
Hewing immortal strokes, but shall the ghosts
Of heroes never walk our milder earth?

IV

After eleven o'clock of November eleventh
We said, *Thank God, we'll build a fire at last!*
Tore the revetments out of ancient trenches,
Kindled a blaze and searched for cigarettes,
Queried, *Well, now, do you reckon the rolling-kitchens*
Will manage to get up? When do we eat?
And went to sleep while bells and whistles cheered
The paper fluttering in a cloud, and people
Shook very clean hands in victorious New York.

Heroes are muddy creatures, a little pale
Under two days' beard with gritty mouths that mumble

Oaths like the Ancient Pistol; or opening cans
Of messy beef with brittle bayonets;
Or winding spiral leggins with eyes alert
For cockle-burrs. Or lanky six-foot men
Earnestly learning to dig with six-inch shovels;
Or tired boys in a trench where shells pursue
Heeding only the frost with a flimsy blanket
Pulled over head and ears. Cramped forms in a dugout
Vomiting smell of gas. Delirious corporals
Tearing at bloody bandages. Captains in rusty
Trench-coats mending broken cigars. Dead men
Wrapped in blankets and earth under wooden crosses.
Living and dead have different tongues for war.

The Living Speak:

THE COLONEL

The men did well. Who would have thought that green
Recruits would face machine-gun fire and crawl
Forward in flanking groups like veterans?
Division staff's another wobblier thing.
Why did they wait till 3 A.M. to give
Their damned old orders? Why did they make me put

The regimental P.C. off to the left?
Why did they send advance guard orders when
I'd told them that my front was held in force?
Why didn't they let me attack the second morning?
When I sent word again and again that I
Was ready to go. There might have been a chance
For a silver star. But now it's back to the cavalry!

THE MAJOR

That damned patrol was foolishness, I knew.
I couldn't tell a lieutenant that. I couldn't
Say, *Yes, of course, you'll never get that gun,*
And never get back alive with only fifteen
Men and such halfway plans. But the Colonel says . . .
West Pointers make me sick. Well, anyway,
We didn't get lost like the third battalion did,
And we got the gun at last. Oh, war is hell,
But cognac softens it around the edges.

COMPANY COMMANDER

Playing God for two hundred men is a snap
Until the battle starts and the scoundrels go

Two hundred different ways. I somehow remember
Bullets nicking the turf beside my wrist,
But mostly I was too busy to be scared.
What I hate worst is the job of writing letters
Back to the mothers and wives of dead men, telling
What noble fellows they were. And so they were.
But how can I say that Corporal Bell's last words
Were these: *Come on, you son-of-a-bitch?* I want
Most of all in this world a thick steak, rare,
French fried potatoes and my Greensboro paper.

A FIRST LIEUTENANT

Why should they have lived, those German gunners, after
They killed Benfield and Clary, Adams and Robertson,
And my good old Sergeant McLarty? War takes guts.
They had guts. We had more. And my rough-neck soldiers
Made them eat dirt. But somehow I'd like to see
What Germany looks like. I wonder if a man
Could get transferred to the Army of Occupation?

SERGEANT SPEAR

I know what killed Lieutenant Clark; it warn't
No Dutchman's bullet. It come from the rear. I know
How Corporal Weinstein got blowed up. It warn't
No Dutchman's shell. I know how Ballington,
The dirty slob, got wounded in the leg.
I done it when the bastard started to run
Just as the third platoon was ordered up.
I know a hell of a lot. But I ain't a-goin' to tell.

CORPORAL SIMMONS

What am I, the son of a Methodist preacher,
A follower of Christ, doing here? Cleaning
Something that looks like blood from my rifle-barrel
And singing: "There is a fountain filled with blood."

LETTER OF GEORGE HART, PRIVATE FIRST CLASS

Well Pa I dont think Germany wants
To fight no more but if they take a crazey
Notion to we will run every D— one of them
Off of the face of the earth. No I dont mean

To do it by myself but you know Wildcats
Scratch like the Devil. Ha! Ha!

VEUVE PROCTOT

Mon Dieu, les sales Américains! Les cochons!
Swallowing the cognac, *comme ça*, demanding bread
When one has no tickets, *vous voyez. Ils disaient*
"BONG JOU' MADEMOISELLE" and winked their eyes
At a poor widow with two sons dead for France.
Alors, one smiles and makes them pay through the
nose.
Ils sont très riches, les Américains, très riches!

MADAME TRUFFOT, WIFE OF THE MAYOR

Comme ils étaient gentils, les Américains! So charming!
The beautiful officer quartered in my home.
But sure to die from a malady of lungs.
On the coldest nights, indeed every night, Monsieur,
He slept with windows open, both completely open,
Both, both open, *le pauvre enfant.*

JEANNE CUGNOT, FERMIÈRE

They paid me many francs, the Americans.
But did they not lose the key to the grange, and laugh
As they left on their camions, shouting insane words?

PRIVATE SMITH

Roses are blooming in Picardy, sang
My buddy, John McLaurin, the night before
We went over the top and he was killed. I think
That roses will bloom on the Hindenburg Line
forever
Out of the breasts of men. Did I read at college
Something of Whitman's, saying, What is the grass?
The grass transpires from the white breasts of young
men.
And roses bloom in the vigilant hearts of friends.

THE DEAD SPEAK:

AN AIRMAN

Return, over the autumn flats, return,
O squadrons of the sky, return from depths
Of blue and pierceable air of France and clouds

That once were wing and wing with us above
The concave gulf of battle. Squadrons, return!
Flash back your thousand circling glittering blades!
Upward your beaks, hurl up your Valkyrie shouts!
Obey, ye dead, the gathering call and keep
A comrade's tryst. Say whether I have fallen!
My death was fair. Far-diving over Conflans,
I drove the enemy home. He fled with speed
But speed still less than mine, until too late
I saw the triple Black Cross ambush plunge,
The fiery river of bullets rending the wood
And then my breast. But fallen? I have not fallen!
My death was pure as flame, and was a flame
To all the watching earth, when what was dross
Blazed toward the dust that never will coop this heart.

A CAPTAIN

From the camp among the pines to the banks of Meuse
True men had followed me. My bidding made
The rifles leap to shoulder when the word
Was forward; then how deft and quick the stir
Of wheeling squads that melted to a column,

Above their caps the steady rifles floated,
Slanting in even lines. The hob-nailed feet
Crunched on the road with a nameless savage murmur.
Bronze faces that were mine, O steady lips,
Young faces crying, *Lead, O lead! We follow!*
Have I not led you then? My death was only
A last salute to you as you passed on.
For on one morning when the word was forward,
First I kept the commander's place and watched
Impatiently your bayonets far ahead.
Thus following you, I lifted up my eyes
Against a wood that smote you as you climbed
The deadly hill of Ronvaux; saw you wavering,
Torn, and huddled where the cross-fire licked
Your brown thin ranks. And then the hour was mine.
I could not bid you then to lead, but sprang
Where all could see, taking from limp dead hands
A soldier's rifle, waved the foremost ranks
Up and on, and saw, before the steel
Kiss of the bullet pierced my side, bronze faces
Following, marching on, the faces I loved,
And took a captain's death, salute to you.

AN ARTILLERYMAN

Missing, was all they said. They could not find
The body that was mine, for the counter-fire
Searched through the battle-fog and struck our guns.
I heard the great shell rustling, with its point
Screaming toward me, and knew it bore my name,
But slammed the breech and sent my last shot home
Before oblivion took me, and the winds
Fluttered the cells that were my body once.
Missing I am not where my comrades gather
Lovingly calling my name for old time's sake.

AN UNKNOWN SOLDIER

Out of the earth that covers me, a pall
Flung by anonymous hands of men, I cry:
Not in vain, O States, not in vain the blood!

V

And now the tide ebbs west again. We are going
Home; we are homeward bound with music
Prouder than when we came and sad but rich
With memories of battle. We who were young

Are older now from death in a foreign land
Met and passed by. Remembering many comrades
We are coming home, fewer than once we were.
After the pilgrimage this is given to us,
Only to say we came with rifles once
Over the sea to a foreign battle, faced
The stranger's bullets, the cold and rain, and worse;
Only to learn what only the soldier knows,
Men find their country beautiful afar.

A flight of gulls! Sand streaks in the green
Tumbling waves! O greener pines! O Carolina!
Sweetly sail, ship in the harbor, home.
That is Fort Sumter — veterans hail a veteran —
Yonder the Battery, yonder the Charleston
Docks and the crowding faces. This is my own countree!
And June beats hot on spacious trains — we are going
Home through a landscape strange. We had never known
It was like this. Trees . . . earth . . . sky.

CONVERSATION IN A BEDROOM

By the waters of Thames or Meuse in another world
I lay me down and slept. By Cumberland
Now in a newer world there is no sleep.
In a square room, pent up with a ticking clock,
Fear drives me on to midnight. Fear
Booms up in measured corners where the boards
And bricks decline more gradually than I
Into their sleep of dust. It is easy to die
For me who am not made of wood or rock.
Minutes fall and flow. On a tousled pillow
Loudly the pulse ticks out my hours of life.
In the brain, numb and secret, insomnia breeds
A throng of bastard monsters. Sleep will not come
For him who counts the sheep or walks the numerals
Tiptoeing up the hundreds. Even to whisper
Under the breath and in the brain old charms
Will not suffice. I have no drug to make
The thinker stop his thinking. Thought remains
An undimensional point that cannot be

Divided or ignored. But there are words
Of poisonous make to feed the poisoned soul.
The bed shakes with horrors. The prurient ear
Remembers ghastly whispers out of the past—

And so you see the medical student put
The nigger's hand, cut-off, inside her bed
Where the sheets parted. They stood outside and,
listened
Half an hour maybe, giggling and whispering,
Then one of 'em put his ear against the door
To follow the joke. He heard a noise,
A sort of animal growling. They opened the door
And found the lights on, found that girl half-nakea
Sitting up in bed with her eyes popping out,
Gnawing that there nigger's hand . . .

Have I not eaten obscene food? Have I waited
For dead men behind closed doors? Have I parleyed
with ghosts,
Loquacious sepulchers diked out in linen,
And yet insist on living? There was a street

Walled up with stony faces, averted eyes,
Garrotting me with sneers —

Why, old ex-service
Nut, why what are you after now that the treaty
Ought to be signed but it's all messed up and jobs . . .
She said, "You'll have to buy an overcoat."
I said, "I've spent my money on railroad fare,
And Treaties of Peace and other perishable rot.
I guess I'll wear my army overcoat."
He said, benignly posed like the annual convention
Of Y.M.C.A. Secretaries, "Well, what are your
Qualifications?" I said, "Qualifications?
In the army I learned the Impossibles."
He said, "We'll file your application." I said,
"Thank you, sir," and walked out buttoning tarnished
Buttons and swinging O.D. sleeves with a yellow V,
Meaning fodder for moths and spider-webs.

Have I prayed to God? Am I washed in the Blood
of the Lamb
In vain? I am red with sin. Or is it the flesh
Raw and stained with my own blood that shows?

Can blood then wash out blood? I'll have no blood,
But rather the potion of a different magic
To make me whole. God has poor ears. They are
clogged
With pontifical wax. Then what of an antique Devil
Whose clean and pointed ears prick artfully up
At my first softest whisper? Magic conquers
Here while the room is turning, and the brain
Is mettled from its wounds for drugs and fancy
Shadows may beg deliverance of shadows,
And I who sleepless groan beg sweet illusion
Whether from Hell or not. Good Devil, hear!

The walls blur and move, dissolving in cloud.
Night is alive with forms to comfort me . . .

And most a black-browed prince with hat and whip
Like a circus Ringmaster. Now with winning smile
He waits for questions such as hurt lips ask . . .

THE RINGMASTER

Though catalogued as a children's bogy,
A museum fossil, a biblical fogy,

I still retain
Some powers not quite ornamental,
Instincts cunningly transcendental,
And I maintain
A private service, guaranteed,
For invalid souls who are in need
Of losing themselves.
The comforts willingly offered you
May now be viewed. But first, we do
Nothing by halves . . .

EGO

The Faustian contract, I suppose you mean?

THE RINGMASTER

I mean the same.

EGO

The price is still a soul?

THE RINGMASTER

The only indestructible — a currency
That never depreciates. Mine is a one-price service.

EGO

Before conviction the shrewd buyer surveys
The various bargain counters. The modern Faust
Has read much more than black-letter books, and seen
A thousand Helens whirled in motor cars.

THE RINGMASTER

A clever point, I grant. Within this box
A two-reel movie's coiled. I now present
Reel One — Disease of Modern Man — with titles
Rhymed as the fancy indicates. So action!

This is Rupert of the House
Of Rupert, famed in history,
Pondering on his income tax,
Deducting genealogy.

Great-grandfather from a loophole
Potted Choctaws in the thicket;
Rupert, menaced by the Reds,
Scratches the Democratic ticket.

Rupert's mother, D.A.R.;
Rupert's father, U.C.V.;
Rupert, mounting in his car,
Zooms up to God in Rotary.

Grandma Rupert had ten children;
Rupert's father begot five.
All of Rupert's stocks and bonds
Are strained to keep one son alive.

Democracy, a fuddled wench,
Is bought from tousled bed to bed.
Bass voices in white vests defile
The echoes of great voices dead.

While piddlers and poseurs accept
The togas fallen by default,
The people's boredom quite dissolves
An honest cynic's grain of salt.

God is purveyed in little chips,
Snatched at and scattered in a quarrel.

The Church, aware of nakedness,
Parades in posters and a barrel.

The guardians of the public eye
Abhor the sin in which we wallow,
And, wearing double lenses, knit,
Fig-leaves for Venus and Apollo.

Editors in public print
Chastise the younger generation,
Distribute syndicated pap,
Promote the national constipation.

* * *

The tribes of men, like haggled deer
Besieged by microscopic teeth,
Walk haunted by the wolves of space,
And in their blood are spores of death.

The flesh that was love's pillow grows
Malignant bulbs of dreadful life.
The newborn idiot defines
A curse that came from man and wife.

The earth, a tiny pellet, rolls
Among vague balls that once were stars.
And men shrink up to specks while minds
Push back astronomy's utmost bars . . .

EGO

Intolerable pictures of death. I cannot bear
This pain of insignificance. Is there no cure?

THE RINGMASTER

The second reel is much the better. It brings
The picture to a happy ending. Here
Are speaking shadows of delivered men,
And ways and means of sweet deliverance.
Look how they rise, a vitaphonic dream!

A TRAVELER

Look to the roads, O sleeper, from which come
Magnificence and peace. Once Marco Polo
Hated the bickerings of Popes, the daggers
Houseled with golden corruption, and journeyed East.
He bathed at Arzingan, forded steamy rivers
Pebbled with lucent jade; he fingered at Yasdi

Cloths of silk and gold; he knew Ormus, Kashcar,
Yarcan, Kamul, Chinchitalos, and many
Cities stranger than dream, and was received
Into the Great Khan's bosom. So I have traveled,
Feasting on alien glory until I am
Myself no longer, but I have found my life.
The rescue of the wise is only in flight,
And lands are left where strangers may be kings.

THE MYSTIC

In the beginning the Word . . . and in the end.
The hawks of doubt fly over the walls of cities
However they are built. The world is made
Of hidden correspondences that blend
In words like secret music. Hide in the darkness,
Hoarding the Word within thee that is life.

A PROMINENT CITIZEN

Are there still fools who think that the word *service*
Means anything? Why, the public pays for it all,
Even to the advertising. But what fun it is
To count one's self devoted, altruistic,

And gild the bones of stupidity.
Benignant Word, delivering me from books
And the intellectual fripperies loved by women.
At civic luncheons I am a boy again,
Hurling breadcrusts, pouring water in chairs
For unwary bottoms. And on convention days
I put on the gorgeous robes of the Mystic Order
And steep my dry soul in forbidden glories.

A FEMINIST

I have dreamed of woman casting off the yoke,
Delivered from old travail and the curse
Of being only a bauble, an easy chattel.
Typewriters click in my office. The yellow blanks
Of telegraph sheets are the living voices of women
Marching shoulder to shoulder in a new day.
It is true, maybe, that men no longer look
At me. It is true, I have thought, O Liberty,
What crimes are committed in thy name. But now
As I finger the indexed files or stand in the lobbies
Demanding and getting what women want, I am
paid . . .

The beautiful dream of the new woman . . . the world
Made lovely by her. Thus the screeching of old maids
Becomes the poetry of heaven . . . the voice of angels.

FIRST EXPATRIATE

Impossible country of bigots and warped schoolma'ams,
I have left you forever. In Paris a man may think
Without having the neighbors call the police patrol.
One may drink, talk, curse, carry a cane,
Wear spats, grow a moustache, and admire James Joyce
Without being charged with adultery. I live in Paris.

SECOND EXPATRIATE

Until I visited Oxford I never knew
What was wrong with me. Then I adopted
The Oxford accent, and became a gentleman.

THIRD EXPATRIATE

Dada is laughter. Picasso, Cézanne, Matisse
Bring man back to his primitive clownish self,
As I discovered in studying negro sculpture.
Visiting New York once I was amazed

To find Dada laughing in negro music.
Dada, I got the blues, I got the Dada blues.
Black men, I am starving. Make me fertile!

SATYR IN A TUXEDO

Bacchus and Silenus betrayed me,
Paul and Peter caught and waylaid me,
Dunstan and Augustine unmade me
With book and bell.

Corinth and Ephesus deserted me,
Provence and Aquitaine perverted me,
Calvin and Wesley seized and converted me
On pain of hell.

Adopted a Presbyterian snuffle,
Survived a Methodist cloak and muffle,
And came to life in the general scuffle
Of creed on creed.

Displaying now a goat's-foot cockily,
Swigging out of the old flask rockily,

Shoved and yet unbudging stockily,
I prance at need.

BOBBED-HAIR BACCHANTE

Nous n'irons plus au bois;
Les lauriers sont coupés.
But take the hour of joy
And speed on a darkened way
From the dance, the cackling horn,
And the raging raging drumbeat . . .
Nous irons jusqu'au bois.
In the silence, love, the meeting of lips till morn.
To others the dance, the fever of stamping feet.
For us, the darkness, the roadway's open retreat . . .
Nous irons jusqu'au bois. . . .

AN INTELLECTUAL

The tree of my life in Peoria, Illinois,
Was a thin sucker branched from a dying stump.
Transplanted now, I gingerly thrust my roots
Into strange pockets of stone where water lurks,
And thus by finical nourishment I grow.

Out of the broken gospels, out of the desert,
The parched, the shattered temples I heard a voice
Chanting to a strident harp, *Oh*, *come*, *come in*,
Come in under the shadow of this red rock . . .
Whither I come, and solace now my heart
With necrological beauties more permanent
In the round glitter of skulls and rondure of bones
Than all the old disease of life. I crush
Hard stone with nervous bruise on ravished knuckles,
Cool my withered tongue with bitter almonds,
And conquer death with death. For all is said
And will not bear repeating . . . at the world's end.

EGO

Oh, stop the reel. These negative freedoms burn
Like rockets in my brain and then puff out
With falling ashes. Here is no rest or peace.
Take back the promise. Steady the whirling walls
Beyond which, out of this nightmare world, there lie
Green hills where moonlight falls on honest grass
And honest men who sleep or, waking, speak
The tongue I speak and love.

But clocks will strike.

With blithely tortured face he warps the night
In shooting lines. Convulsive blackness crimps
A blasted angular world where fungus growths
Knit pile on pile of horrible beauty splashed
With writhing human smiles. Lights! Lights! I say . . .

Shall ever medicine thee!

The lights are broken.

In a cackle of stentorian type I see
Immense tongues wagged from fleshless lips
And (TIME!) they prophesy corruption (TIME!)
From which strange flowers (TIME!) shall bloom
With fruitage (TIME!) that shrivels (TIME!) my soul . . .
Oh (TIME!) give me release from searing (TIME!)
Blackness (TIME!). Bring not this grain to (TIME!)
The harvest (TIME!) and fly the bearded sheaves.
Fly from the wrath of God *O lente lente*
(TIME!) *currite noctis equi.* Still
I'll buckle the heart with steel and smiling . . .

(TIME!)

* * *

Who comes and proves that you are suddenly perishing
Let him be choked on his own blue-prints of hell.
Let his tongue itch with death, a furious cancer.
Let him bite his nails in the lone eyries of skyscrapers,
Invaded by personal devils.

Who comes with poisons,
Mental unguents and glittering antitoxins,
Clap him in the mortuary. Hang him by the ears,
Pendulous among the stiffs. Let him joke with the
corpses.
Let him be burned in the crematory at last
Totally to ashes. Then bring a broom and shovel.

No perfume either.
Only the light of dawn.

No gables burn, nor is it a dragon's breath
Blazing in eastern woods. It is no light
Of strangers' weapons clashing at eastern windows
And no false fire of hell.
This is the dawn!

And dawn's no fragile wonder. Dawn is a whistle
Blown for the Judgment Day each morning at five,
And out of perilous sleep the calm mind rises.
Dawn is a headline tossed on a sunny step,
The voice of the burly nations. Dawn is a woman
Lifting round arms before a mirror. Dawn
Is a child quickly alive with new imperatives,
A friend crossing the grass with eager feet and calling
Under the window where you sleep, *Oh, come,*
Come down. I have news or you. It is morning!

THE BREAKING MOULD

"O KING," the atheling said, "how the time of man
Is like to a sparrow's flight from door to door
Of a hall where men sit feasting, and fire is warm.
From cold and darkness it comes. It is safe from weather
A moment only; then into the dim and outward
Winter it flies again. Does a man speak now
A word more certain than this? Does the tale of Christ
Speak a better word? Then I bid thee follow it."

The long-haired thanes were silent in hall, and Aedwin
Stroked at his beard. He took the priest's thin hand
Into both his great ones, hairy and scarred. He bowed
For the blessing of Christ his body, clashing with mail.
The Northumbrian shields upheld an alien captain.
The body of Christ was king in the circle of spears.
And lo, I was seized, marching from Baltic forests,
Or pressing beyond the Danube, the Rhine, or the Seine.
Salty with wash of the fjords, rimy with sea-spray,
I in my great boar-helmet was seized and won

By a lean priest whose eyes were kindling with dreams
Of the blessed Rood. I was gentled with Latin hymns,
Cleansed with holy water and crowned with thorns,
And told to remember a sin I had not known.
The hammer of Thor was fallen forever, and Odin
Looked upon Asgard sadly. Twilight came
With a mild Christian splendor of bells and incense.
The Goths unbuckled the sword. The sons of the Goths
Remembered the saints in stone with arches leaping
Heavenward like my soul from the desolate earth.

But now a hammer shines in the hand of Luther
Nailing the ninety-nine theses on a door
At Wittenberg where sparks fly up. Tyndale
Burns, and Scotland's burning. A voice cries,
I tell thee, Master Ridley, this day we light
A fire, O such a fire, shall burn and never
Shall be put out. Now merry England's burning,
And I, dancing with sinful friends on the village green,
Heard voices crying out of heaven, *Fly!*
Fly from the wrath to come! And as I slept
I dreamed a dream of Beulah Land for which

I fought on Naseby Field, and later sailed
To a land not Beulah Land. With my father's claymore
I still fled sin to the western mountains. There
The hunting-shirts were bowed at Watauga Old Fields,
And Samuel Doak, before King's Mountain, prayed
To the ancient God of battles. Are these not blessed,
The stern lips of mountain men who pray,
Firm in search for God so many a year?
And to me Evangelist came again in the blare
Of a cornet under a canvas tent, a borrowed
Piano tinkling a washed-out music, a sweating
Choir vaguely exalting the youthful blood
Of sinners —

Brother, are you a Christian? Are you
Washed in the Blood? Oh, Brother, sinful Brother,
Come while the choir sings Number Seventy-nine
And give me your hand. God bless you, Brother. God
Bless you, young man. Will there be any stars
Any stars in my crown when at evening . . .

When at evening, I, a man conceived in sin,
Walked, unthoughtful of sin, I saw overhead

Vega, against the murk of space, and Mars,
A reddish bulb swung closer to this globe
By a few million miles. And Ursa Major
Hurled west against the beating of my heart
Forever. I said, the sun will rise and dawn
Will break again forever. The moon will turn
Its dry face toward the clutching earth, and men
Will walk as I have walked and ask the same
Clean question of a God that never answers . . .

When at evening I, a man conceived in sin,
Walked, not professing sin, I felt a cloud
Darken the windows of my brain, and death
Looked coarsely in. I said, this mortal plasm
Living by process of all centuries
Not yet has died. The seed is old as man,
Remainder and sum of many bodies, soul
Of infinite souls, an indestructible life.
Then say not, death, I shall not clench this hand
To-morrow . . . to-morrow I shall not see this sky.
Say not to-morrow this bright urgency
Of looks and words must pass. Oh, come away, death!

I who have had no ending cannot know
What it is to end. I who have had no beginning
Know life only. Beyond, by either way,
Is God, whose answer has not come to men
But in the rumors of men — a gypsy race
Who flaunt their pride in legends of old glory
Half-forgotten, repeated as a charm
For comfort's sake when wind blows cold and death
Stands at the road's edge, a shadow beckoning *Stop.*

But still men dare to speak for God and shape
Their fumbling answers into a mould to keep
The quick proud spirit against the outer dread
Of spaceless terrible things. God is the mould
So many times cast off, so many times
Clay on the wheel again. For if ever the soul
Moves in its changeful dreams, the mould must
break.
It is my restless soul that stirs. It is
My soul that will not be contained in the dead
Plaster that other hands have made. It is cramped
And like a child within the womb it must

Begone from that which gave it life. It rends,
It cleaves its way, and there is agony.

But if I pass you by, O House of God,
It is not now in scorn. I would not sit
In the seat of the scornful or walk in the way of sinners.
But men are greater than the house they build
Even the House of God. And the prayers of men
Are mightier than the altars where they bow
Their wounded heads in one eternal wish.
I seek the joy of life. I seek the God
Who will not tame the manliness of men.

Three men am I. And one with pagan blood
Startles at dawn to find no sword at his side,
No hound to answer his horn, no charger ready,
No ashen spear by the wall, no throng of men
Bearded, shining with mail, in the smoky hall,
No noise of the feasting of gods in high Asgard.
And he says in his teeth: Now who has bewildered me
A thousand years with a doctrine of strange tongues?
Who clad me in strange garments? What smooth saws

Were whispered into my ear by Eastern voices?
What were the swarthy faces, what the drug
That sank me into slumber? I am not
Of the blood of Hebrews. Who gave me over to Hebrews?
After a thousand years I have not learned
The voice of the Hebrew God or the Hebrew way.

The second man of me is Puritan,
Who learned of a godly mother the Ten Commandments
And read the Good Book through at the age of twelve,
Chapter by chapter. The hymns of country choirs
Haunt my tongue. The words of stately men
Speaking from ghostly pulpits forbid me still
From shameful things. And youthful prayers arise
Unbidden to my lips in hours of dread.
Woman is sacred still, and wine is a mocker,
The words of God are written in the Book
Which I will keep beloved though earth may speak
A different language unto those who read her.

The third man was born to weigh the sun
And love the clean cool sureties of matter.

Whatever God is, this man does not guess.
He is content to know what all things do
Or can be made to do. How little is man,
He thinks, reckoning the life of stars, and yet
How easily things beneath the stars may serve
This little man's great will. No question shows
The cause behind a cause, for ever there are
Unmeasured causes still. He had rather walk
The observant friend of the world as it looks to be,
And move with it among all active things,
Using them all, or maybe used by them.
And if he die — why, many men have died!
And what is God? Well, what He is, He is —
Some Great Electron, not yet trapped or seen,
But there or not, whatever our debates.

In elder days than these men saw the gods.
Red-bearded Thor in a goat-pulled chariot came
To Thialfi's hut. Men sat at meat with the god,
Tearing the goat-flesh, jesting over the mead
Till the rafters rang and the gold-haired maidens laughed.
And once on a misty dawn by a northern ford

A ferryman answered a stranger's call, received
Into his boat an old man, one-eyed, gray-cloaked.
The shore was touched. And then the charmed man saw
The gnarled figure straighten and tower. Fog
Swirled round the breast of Odin. The golden voice
Spoke farewell to a man who sat with oars
Poised in a breathless trance. And on that spot
He raised a cairn of stones and slew a horse,
Sprinkling the blood while solemn runes were chanted.

Evangelist, you who called to me on the curb
And waved an inviting hand toward the vacant seat
Beside you in the car, hear this my question:
How can three alien men be reconciled
In one warm mind that like the sparrow flies
In a great hall lit for feasts and the laughter of men,
And would be glad before it goes forever
Out of the opening door? Oh, give me a scroll
Written anew, for where I pass are lions
Walking chainless and devils that will not flee.

The mould breaks, and God must arise again.
And you, my known or unknown friend, believe

That my notion of God is less than my notion of you,
For somehow man encloses the only God
With whom I dare be intimate. I have heard
The brave laughter of men who were fated to die
And cannot think that God surpasses them
In finite beauty — and my world is finite.
And you, beloved, it is no April fire
That brings my lips to yours again. It is
No sudden springtime burning in the veins
That soon must slacken. This is the deepest flame
Ever given to man, the love of life
Summed up in you, for what we have learned of God
Is not yet more mysterious, is not
More powerful a life than this we share,
Companions, lovers, in one destiny.

EPITHALAMION

I

Now while the West is thunder and the broad
Hurry of wind in the oak and hackberry boughs
Crashes and shatters; now while the lightning breaks
The tumbled darkness, clogged with fluttering leaves;
Now while the endless rain is dashed in gusts
Against our windows, — now we awake from sleep
And, fixed with a wild dread, we startle erect,
Crying, "Is it a storm?"

It is only a storm!

And then the warm hands fold in the darkness, then
Each knows that each is there, and the flame of lightning
Blazons only the passionate faces of lovers,
Saying, *Only a storm.* . . . And storms will pass,
And we shall stay in our firm element
Of human love, our *primum mobile.*

We have known this darkness and this storm of old.
Lady, it is the death of the year that speaks

In this familiar wind and rain — the turn
Of autumn into winter. Now the earth
Tips gently in its ceaseless whirl, and stars
Glide on their winter courses. Soon the sleet
Will dance across the frozen grass. The snow
Will pile small soundless drifts across the ledge
Of this our window. Sun will be far and weak.
And under the breath we'll measure life and think
Now, oh, now, we are older by a year
And shall be older still, not young again,
And smile a little ruefully, and sigh,
"So many years" and "Time goes on forever."
But when the eternal janitor has swept
The stairs to this our refuge, this small heaven,
Will he erase, with other dust, the print
Of mounting feet like ours that came and went
On lovers' errands? Will no echo stay
Of these our voices in the walls that bound
Our lovers' meetings? Will the final spring,
Unsealing after the storm the red-bud blooms,
Rustle of maple leaves, and the sheen of grass,
Unseal no lovers' eyes to sight of us

Who came and went another spring?

Look not

For any ghostly consequence. Our love
Is ours only — the old way of the world
That in itself completes itself and asks
No doctrine or memorial but its own.

Morning will come and we shall not be here,
Lady, whose eyes like mine awake,
Remembering in silence that we still
Are here who cannot always . . . always . . . be.

But if we cannot always waken thus
Remembering the days that make us one,
Let us remember now, let us remember
Morning by morning, night by night, the love
That, coming once, has come to us forever.

For us the flying months, forever April,
Take back no youth we cannot take again
In giving by the touch of hands or lips
*New morning to our love. For morning **is***

A presence that we keep within ourselves
Translating and remembering all we are.

And shall I now translate these simple words
Into a bolder epithalamion?
The talk of blood, tears, agony, and doubt,
The patterns of the outward world, the din
Of old historic moments—all must dwindle
Into a sultry whisper, and I shall come
As a young man seeking your lips and crying Love!

II

Northward the Tennessee under stars or sunlight
Flows unmindful of names and lines of men.
It was not drawn by the compass. It will not follow
Any map but its own. It will seek its own,
Its northward pathway where in the dawn of the world
The broad earth, cleft and yielding, brought it home
To the strange Ohio's breast. And the swift Ohio
Came in the dawn of the world to a southward meeting.
Now they are poured together. The rivers are one.

You are Ohio. I am Tennessee.
And in being faithful to you I have been unfaithful
Maybe, this once, to my own. I forgot the looks
Of the Tennessee girls whose ways were sweet enough
For an early spring, for a young man mad with spring,
Drunken with smell of locust-clusters, drugged
With the subtle filtering odor of honeysuckle.
Moonlight loosened my tongue. It was easy to look
On the warm white throats of Southern girls. It was
easy.
To hear soft laughter on a vine-thick porch.
But I was a willing traitor when you came.

And why, you know I know. The small proud head,
Carried erect and firm; the thinking eyes
So dark and yet so clear with bright intention;
Lips curling easily into a smile; a body
Lithe and quick as a bird's and just as restless;
The strange clipped Northern speech; the hurrying step
Of those who dwell by Erie's shore and take
The lake-wind in their blood and the blue water
Beating on shores where men's dreams rise in steel.

That was your being and is still. You might
Be carved in stone, a daughter of winds and lakes,
But stone could not record what I know best,
The supple, reaching mind that leaps and conquers,
Vital and passionate after knowledge, spurning
The weak and easy, an intellectual flame.

Ohio girl, so new to me, so lovely,
I have taken you to my father's house, a stranger.

But was there maybe an elder meeting when,
Guarded by men in blue, the ragged lines
Of weary men in gray had halted at noon
By an old Ohio farmhouse. Shade was thick
And gentle by the gate. And then there came
A dark-eyed girl with pity in her glance,
Pity and love for a tired boy in gray
Who took with grateful lips the cup she poured
Of water, for love's sake, and looked his thanks,
And plodded on, when the sharp bugle called,
With a wistful backward smile. And did you then
Smile, too, across the gulf of war, and know

That bayonets cannot prison love. Love is
More proud and strong than armies with their banners.

And was there still an earlier meeting? Say,
If you remember in your blood a meeting
Brief by the Frisian coast, when the fair-haired Goths
Came a-harrying over the path of the whale.
Bright was the hall. The herald strode in the folk-stead.
Good to see was the man of the Goths when he came
Lifting his hand, unlocking his breast:

O King!

Shelter of earls, to thee now offer the Goths
Peace in the burg. Plunder they will not bear
Hence in their ships if thou art minded for peace.

Young was the herald of Goths. The light of his eyes
Burned in the crowded hall. And the eyes of a girl
Met his warm through the spears. The daughter of kings
Was not loath to look. But wroth were the Frankish men.
Eyes had spoken in vain. That day was battle.

There have been meetings unfulfilled and partings
Sealed with pledges under a castle window,

Longings unfulfilled when the clear horn sang
Challenge to battle waged in a foreign land.
And on his brest a bloodie crosse he bore
But on his arm his own liege lady's scarf
In deare remembrance . . .
On a later morn
The bugles played our reveille for France
And I was gone from you to a foreign field.

But have come back! Fulfillment of old vows
And broken meetings lies within a touch,
A look, a word, the silence of our hearts
Until our single room becomes the world.

Come now, though Muses are not left to sing
In sweet and pagan names the day of love,
Though ancient rites escape our fostering,
And boys and girls may take no blossom trove
From April boughs whereof
Garlands we plucked when youth was at its spring;
Though viol and rebeck may no longer play
For largesse of this morn, nor dancers move

With music to the house where we must stay,
Yet Love, awake, for still it is our bridal day.

Awake and come to windows where the night
Is gone and takes the storm, the powerful spell
That once it worked on us, but now delight
Kindles the tongue of every morning bell.
Awake and answer well
With thy red lips and all thy lovely might.
Enclose me with thine arms and kiss away
Old fevers that we breathed in love's despite,
And breathe a world where we can longer stay,
And wake, my Love, for still it is our bridal day.

Open the door whereat my love will go
To this the festival so long ordained.
Let be the music that ye long have feigned
For bridals that ye know,
And let the hills another music sound
From old and stubborn ground.
Let the long street a solemn music speak
And larger beauties break

From this wide world that is our marriage room,
And April grass and every April bloom,
And Hymen cry and now your joyance make,
And drink the skies' sweet influence while ye may.
Go forth, my Love, for still it is our bridal day.

RESURRECTION

"I AM the Resurrection and the Life."
Sayeth the smell of wild plum-blossoms tossed
Fragrantly on the scragged hill, a cloud
Swaying the mild traveler, commanding peace.
After the whirl of false dreams, after the flux
Of melting apparitions, I return
Unto this earth, this rock, this hill, this sky
Where as a boy I walked, knowing no roof
Of stars, no wall of cloud, no wave of hills,
No cry of birds, no air, no home but this,
Loving no other city but my own,
After the pilgrimage fully seen at last . . .
With hoof-thuds on the dust and scraping the rocks
The slow mules strain back against the creak
Of moving wheels. The brake screams on. It comes,
The giant corpse of a tree still green with moss,
An unlopped bough yet ignorant of death
Flittering its leaves, bobbing a crooked arm
To the gradual fumbling rhythm of the load.

RESURRECTION

The teamster, careless as God, unsnarls his whip,
Cracks the long lash and chirrups, gathers the reins
Coolly like God and rides the shorn log home.
"I am the Resurrection and the Life,"
Sayeth the mouth that blooms, commanding peace.
"Be still," sayeth the teamster's quiet body,
Borne with unsullen glance above the dust.
Cast not your tortured flesh beneath the wheels
Where death rolls on to other shapes of life,
And all that passes is the pantomime
Of all that flows within and looks without.
Suffer the breath of the wild plum-bush to run
Into the brain, the parching fiber of brain.
The wild plum-blossoms fiercely lift their life,
A momentary beauty, rich from a thin soil,
Till the hard hill is translated. I am not dead
As yet or am arisen who see the gnarled
Boughs of the plum-tree burst into sudden white
Like the fallen bosom of Christ that buds again,
Like the dead words of Christ that flower again.
"I am the Resurrection and the Life,"
Sayeth the slender form of the young girl

Whose hour is April — and she stands alone
Upon the platform of an ancient stair.
Her hand is at the door. She lifts the bolt,
With warm inevitable motion urging the wood
Backward and open into a crumbling mansion
Where ghosts salute and vanish. April attends her,
Month of the swelling seed that break the husk
Of rotting silence where her body moves.
The white pillars are living. The house quivers
With clash of opening windows on the world.
"I am the Resurrection and the Life,"
Sayeth the crumbling step of a lordly man
Whose back the winters cannot bow, but still
He lifts old slumbrous eyes against the heights
Unscalable, where gray importunate captains
Beckon, to meet new dooms, their risen hosts.
His eyes must hunt the fox on uplands pitched
Above the broken streets, and while the horn
Winds in his brain a lovely blast he goes
Crying with swift unutterable looks,
Remember me! O proud young sons, believe!
For whosoever liveth and believeth in me

Shall not compose the fallen dust but flow
Into my beauty, an everlasting flame . . .
And I'll remember thee, for now the horn
Winds in my brain a summons as of dawn
To where the fox, the wild fox spring, still runs
An everlasting flame across the years.

Downward from hills, and pacing the long street,
I move where April moves and strews the way
With echoes of old springs unknown, not lost.
After the pilgrimage, the bloody wrath, the death
Of many false gods, worshiped in many lands,
I pace again the long street, bringing the spoil
Of this my only triumph, trumpeting news
At every door. O stranger and my friend,
There are no garlands and no banners hung
Across the streets of home. There are no crowds
To clap their feverish hands and shout the glory
Here of our permanent victory. But here
The power is and glory. Here arise,
Like exhalations out of earth and stone,
The walls we build, the roofs that cover us,

Founded upon the bosoms of the dead.
Beneath us tier on tier are locked in mould
The bones of those who fought and loved here once
Like us who fight and love. Builders of mounds
Have given their secret unto earth and gone
A thousand years. Under these floors and fields
The Red Men are who walked as blithe as we
In this warm sun. And here their enemies,
The tall men, lie within the land they won.
And now the flesh of warriors, builders, friends,
White man and negro, slave and master, thief
And hero, conquered and conqueror,
Makes rich the ground whereon we build and move
To our own conquest, no less hard than theirs,
Perhaps not less heroic. Out of their death
Leaps now our life, out of decay the flash
Of this high moment, out of the shadow, light.

Pacing the long street where summer waits
Behind a curtain of unuttered days,
I meet the romance of my other lives
A thousand times. If ever of old I heard

Some tale of that Arcadia where the gods
Became as shepherds piping the songs of men
And crowned their temples with our mortal wreaths.
I have known them here on days of crystal air
When clouds raced over the pastures and the hills
Were buoyant green. The clatter of linden-shields
That ceased at Maldon sounds by the Tennessee waters
And Byrhtnoth guards the ford. The horn of Roland
Trails its blast in the Cumberland hills. The spears
Of mediæval twilight cluster here. The Grail
Burns red above the housetops. Holy, holy,
Holy chime the bells, holy the hour,
Joyful the traveler when he lifts his eyes
Returning from far lands and knows his home.

Come now, stranger and friend, the lights bloom up,
And we are here who never thought to meet
Again in any world. We did but make
A circle out of time to kill our fear—
But now have courage. Come while the Iron Age
With pomp of horns and smoking frankincense
Laughs at the gate and time is yet of spring.

For rumors of spring are at our ears. They are borne
Forever before us. Whatever lies in earth
From which I was born, to which I will surely pass;
Whatever was in the seed of my beginning,
Different from other men, yet the sum of many,
And the sum of causes backward to the first cause;
Whatever the flame, ashes, pain, or splendor of man,
Glory or disaster, tumult of the present moment
And all past moments — this I accept or give,
Mortal or immortal in you or me, speaking
As a voice from graves or from men's own windows,
Hurled up from pavements, vocal where men gather,
Blown like dust or stars into the live heart beating.

EPILOGUE

FIRE ON BELMONT STREET

HE was a worthy citizen of the town.
"Where is the fire?" he babbled as he ran.
"The fire! The fire!" Spat between pursy breaths
He dropped his question, stuck his gross right hand
Against his watch-chain, ran, and stared, and sobbed,
Out Belmont Street? My God, that's where I live!
Stumbling with slow fat feet and tragic breath
While roaring sirens passed upon the wind.
And then I heard (What laughter!) blobs of heels
Pecking the night with hurry. Poor staccato,
Dragging a million feeble stumps across
The easy pavements while the flames went up,
Gobbling the roofs and sky. Beneath was earth.
Steady against all shouting, ground was waiting
Forever subtle, old. But walls dissolved
And houses quaked with Fire until I could
Endure no more, but ran, as clamorous
As all the plump mad mob, shouting like them:

"The fire," I cried. What fire? No gables burn,
Nor is that redness some unusual dawn
Sprawled against moonrise, nor a dragon's breath
Spurted from some old sewer you forgot,
Nor ghosts of Red Men that your fathers knew,
Come back with devil-medicine to bombard
Your bungalows. Choctaw and Cherokee
Lie where the spitting Decherd rifles planted
Under the Tennessee grass, their tired bones.
The fire! What fire? Why God has come alive
To damn you all, or else the smoke and soot
Have turned back to live coals again for shame
On this gray city, blinded, soiled, and kicked
By fat blind fools. The city's burning up?
Why, good! Then let her burn!

But I'll say more,

Remembering other odds, a narrow place,
A shock of arms, a cry of gables burning.
And there were gathered in that long grim room
Of warriors sixty who called Hnaef their lord,
Who saw the gray wolf creeping in the wood
And heard the grind of linden shields afar;

Surrounded were, yet held the door and died
While the strange light of swords and helmets made
The place like day.
But who will stand tonight,
Holding this other door against the press
Of brazen muscles? Who can conquer wheels
Gigantically rolled with mass of iron
Against frail human fingers? Who can quench
The white-hot fury of the tameless atoms
Bursting the secret jungle of their cells?
Oh, who can stay or ever chain the dull
Gnaw of the fiery smoke, eternally settling
Into the beating heart? There is no fire?
Only, perhaps, the breath of a Southern wind
That I have known too well in many a summer,
Drying the pulse, stopping the weary pulse,
Blowing the faint blood back in the curdled veins
Till there is no way to think of what might be
Better or worse. Yet maybe it were better
Climbing the tallest hill to cry at night:
"Citizens, awake! Fire is upon you, fire
That will not rest, invisible fire that feeds

On your quick brains, your beds, your homes, your
steeples,
Fire in your sons' veins and in your daughters',
Fire like a dream of Hell in all your world.
Rush out into the night, take nothing with you,
Only your naked selves, your naked hearts.
Fly from the wrath of fire to the hills
Where water is and the slow peace of time."

There is a place where beech-trees droop their boughs
Down-slanting, and where the dark cedars grow
With stubborn roots threading the lichened rocks.
There the smooth limestone benches, rubbed
By warm primeval streams, yet hold the crystal
Forms of dead life. There on a summer's evening
The screech-owl quavers and unseen July-flies
Trill their thin songs. And there my father said
Pointing a low mound out to me, "My son,
Stand on this Indian's grave and plainly ask,
Indian, what did you die for? And he'll say,
Nothing!"

EPILOGUE

So was it! So it is!

What did you die for? Nothing indeed nothing!
The seed of the white man grows on Indian graves,
Waxing in steel and stone, nursing the fire
That eats and blackens till he has no life
But in the fire that eats him. White man, remember,
Brother, remember Hnaef and his sixty warriors
Greedy for battle-joy. Remember the rifles
Talking men's talk into the Tennessee darkness
And the long-haired hunters watching the Tennessee
hills
In the land of big rivers for something.